D1716793

Children's book author **Cécile Jugla** knows that the best way to learn about and understand science is by observing and doing experiments ... which is why she wrote and designed the *There's Science in* series, full of exciting discoveries.

Creator of the Cité des Enfants, and former director of the Palais de la Découverte science museum in France, **Jack Guichard** loves to bring scientific principles to life, making them accessible to everyone.

Laurent Simon illustrates books for children (and grown-ups, too), and sometimes he also writes them. He particularly likes to illustrate science books, though.

First American Edition 2024
Kane Miller, A Division of EDC Publishing
Copyright © 2020 by Editions NATHAN, SEJER, Paris — France,
Édition orignale: *La science est dans le papier*

For information contact:
Kane Miller, A Division of EDC Publishing
5402 S 122nd E Ave, Tulsa, OK 74146
www.kanemiller.com
www.paperpie.com

Library of Congress Control Number: 2023938253
Printed and bound in France
1 2 3 4 5 6 7 8 9 10

ISBN: 978-1-68464-756-9

FSC
MIX
Paper
FSC® C022030

All photos © Shutterstock

If you make fun of me, I'll crumple!

There's
Science in
PAPER

Text by **Cécile Jugla** and **Jack Guichard**

Illustrations by Laurent Simon

Kane Miller
A DIVISION OF EDC PUBLISHING

Contents

GET TO KNOW YOUR PAPER

Do you have a sheet of plain printer paper in front of you? OK! Let's take a closer look.

When you shake a sheet of paper it makes a lot of noise

What shape is your sheet of paper?

round   oval   rectangle   square   hard to say

Answer: rectangle

Describe your paper...

smooth

rough

matte

shiny

scented

bumpy

heavy

When you shake a folded sheet, there is less noise, and the sound is more muffled

8

Your sheet of paper was:

harvested
in a field

manufactured in
a factory

produced by
a kangaroo

Answer: Paper is manufactured from wood in a factory called a paper mill.

Which of the objects below
is not made of paper?

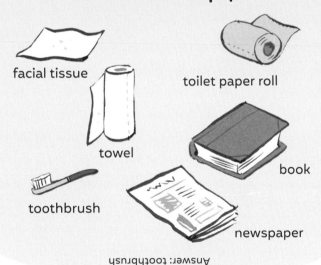

facial tissue

toilet paper roll

towel

book

toothbrush

newspaper

Answer: toothbrush

Good work!
You've learned a lot about paper.
Turn the page to find out more.

HOW IS PAPER MADE?

Shine a flashlight behind your sheet of paper.

You can see through it! There are gray spots.

What are these spots ❓

Fibers, sort of microscopic threads, hooked together.

Did you know?
Paper can also be made from fabric, plants, and even horse poop—they all contain fibers!

What is the paper made of ❓

Small pieces of wood chips, which are made of cellulose fibers.

How are the fibers arranged in paper ?

The tear is **straight** because it follows the direction of the fibers: most are arranged lengthwise.

The tear goes **across** to join the direction of the fibers. You can also try with a facial tissue: it's even more spectacular!

 Well done! You've learned about the structure of paper.

WRITE A SECRET MESSAGE

Write a message in pencil. Don't press down too hard.

The message is written in the left corner.

The candy is in the vase.

The sheet is folded once, then folded again.

♪♪ Ta-da!

The message is invisible.

Why is the message invisible ?

The folded paper is thick. Natural light cannot easily go through the layers of fibers. The paper is **opaque**.

Why does the message appear under a lamp ?

The light from the lamp, which is very strong, goes through the fiber layers. The paper is **translucent**.

Did you know?
If you hold a banknote up to a light, you should see a watermark or faint image ... unless it's counterfeit!

You've got it!
You know that paper can be opaque or translucent to light.

CUT A BANANA WITH PAPER

Cut out a strip of paper from a magazine.

1.5"

Peel the banana like so.

Don't take a bite!

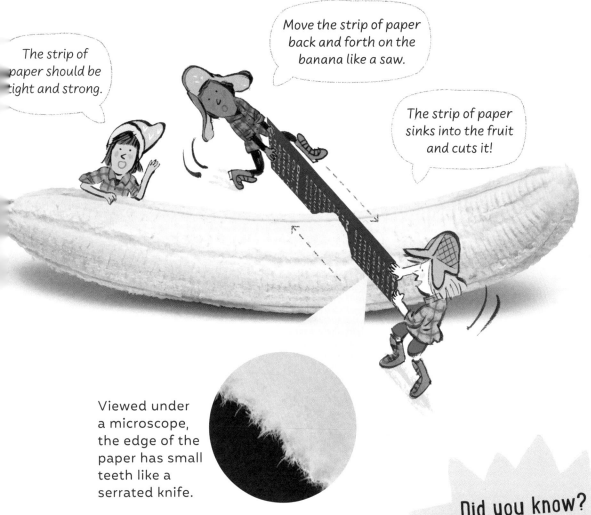

The strip of paper should be tight and strong.

Move the strip of paper back and forth on the banana like a saw.

The strip of paper sinks into the fruit and cuts it!

Viewed under a microscope, the edge of the paper has small teeth like a serrated knife.

How does the paper cut the banana ?

The strip of paper is rigid, like the blade of a knife, and it sinks into the fruit. With its **thin serrated** edge, it **cuts the banana**.

Did you know?
Sometimes you can cut yourself if you slide your finger quickly on the edge of a sheet of paper.

Wonderful! You've learned that the fibers on the edge of paper can cut like a knife.

MAKE A PAPER HAT

You need a sheet of square, thin paper.

Fold the corners from the top to the middle. Press the folds.

Fold up the band that protrudes in front.

A little extra tip

To make the fold sharper, you can press on it with your fingernail.

Fold the strip at the back too.

And the result is ... a beautiful paper hat!

I tried this using a cloth napkin. It doesn't stay folded.

Why does the paper fold better ?

When we **fold** paper, **the paper fibers** inside the fold are **broken**, while those outside are stretched, and so the sheet remains folded.

Great job! You've learned some origami, the art of folding paper, and discovered that you can break the fibers of the paper when you fold it.

MAKE BLOOMING PAPER FLOWERS

Why does the paper bloom in water ?

The water **penetrates** between and into **the crushed fibers** of the paper's fold. This **puffs up** and **straightens** the folded paper. Newspaper fibers absorb the water right away, but white paper is covered with a varnish, so it takes longer.

What a scientist! You have discovered the principle of capillary action, which allows water to circulate in the paper fibers!

WATCH COLORS GROW AND CHANGE

Draw colored dots along the top of a paper towel with felt-tip pens.

0.8 inch

At the bottom, draw lines the same colors as the dots at the top.

Green and black markers work well for this experiment, too.

Dip the bottom edge of the paper towel in white vinegar. Don't let the vinegar touch the lines.

Oh! The vinegar spreads the colors up the paper towel!

White Vinegar

0.2 inches of white vinegar

The colors change too! The green is separated into yellow and blue.

Why do the ink colors separate ?

As the ink travels up the paper towel, the vinegar **draws out** and **separates its colored pigments**. The **lightest** pigments rise the **highest**.

What a good printmaker! You have tested to what extent ink pigments penetrate paper.

MAKE PAPER FLY

What makes paper fly faster or slower ?

With its very small surface, **the ball** offers little resistance to the air, so it **falls quickly**.

1

The folded sheet has a small surface. The air pushes against it and **slows the paper down**.

2

The whole sheet gives the air a large surface to push against, so it **falls slowly!**

3

For the ball: hip, hip, hip …

A little extra tip

If you make a paper plane, it goes even faster. With its pointed shape, it moves through the air easily. It is aerodynamic.

OK! You now understand how to reduce the friction of the air on the paper to speed up its flight.

TEST THE STRENGTH OF PAPER

You will need 4 sheets of legal size paper.

Starting at the bottom, roll each sheet twice, to make a tube.

1.5"

8.5"

Add a piece of tape to hold it in place.

Did you know?
Some furniture is made from cardboard! This very strong cardboard is made of a layer of corrugated cardboard, glued between 2 layers of cardboard.

We're placing the 4 tubes upright.

We're gently adding a book, and another, and another ...

The first book protrudes 0.8 inches over the tubes.

0.8"

The tubes can hold 44 pounds of books!

How does paper hold the weight of books ?

Paper is fragile. But when it's in the shape of a tube—or a cylinder—it becomes more rigid and resistant.

You're an architect! You've proved that a cylindrical shape increases the strength of paper.

MAKE TWO BOOKS STICK TOGETHER

Why don't the books come apart ?

The book pages are made of **rough paper**. They **rub** against each other and **cling to one another**. The more pages you've used, the stronger the link.

A little extra tip

Try the experiment with 2 glossy magazines with smooth and shiny paper. The sheets will slip and separate more easily.

Congratulations! You've discovered the force that causes the sheets of paper to attach to each other. This force is called friction.

MAKE RECYCLED PAPER

You need a small bottle of water.

Cut a sheet of newspaper into small pieces, then soak the pieces in a bowl of water.

Ask an adult to mix the paper and water with an immersion blender

What is paper pulp ?

A **gray, slimy sludge**. The bonds between the fibers of the waterlogged paper have broken. The glue that binds them together has gone into the water.

Strain the pulp for 5 minutes.

Spread the pulp on a dish towel.

Next, fold the cloth over the pulp.

Paper pulp

Dish towel

Tray

Press the pulp hard with a rolling pin.

10 times

The water that comes out of the pulp can be thrown away.

Lift the cloth gently to let the pulp dry.

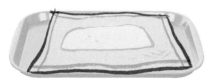

The paper fibers have been pressed and glued together.

Here it is ... recycled paper!

The pulp can be dried in the sun or near a radiator.

Excellent! You have discovered how to recycle paper!